AF351696

RUNE CASTING WORKBOOK

Learning Guide for Reading Runes

Loera Publishing LLC

Rune Casting Workbook
Copyright @ 2019 All rights reserved.

Second Edition December 2021

Without limiting the rights under the copyright reserved above, no part of this book may be reproduced, stored in or introduced into a retrieval system, or transmitted, in any form, or by any means (electronic, mechanical, photocopying, recording, or otherwise) without the prior written permission of Diana Loera and Loera Publishing LLC.
Book piracy and any other forms of unauthorized distribution or use without written permission by Diana Loera/Loera Publishing LLC will be prosecuted to the fullest extent of the law.

Contents

Do I Need to Own Runes to Use This Workbook?

While it is great to already own your runes, the right set may not have called out to you yet – and that is totally fine.

If you do not own a set of runes yet, you can write the symbols on equal size and color pieces of paper and find a small container to store them in.

If you have small flat stones, you can write the symbol on each one using a permanent marker. Use your imagination and find objects that will work. It is totally okay.

The main thing is that you are following the path of your interest and beginning the learning process.

Introduction

Several years ago, I came across runes being read at a Renaissance Faire that was located two states away from my home. I drove back to the faire several times that summer determined to find out more about the runes.

This was before the Internet gained popularity. Finding a book such as this proved difficult. The local library had none. Even local bookstores were limited at that time. I'd sometimes luck out and come across a "New Age" magazine with a small ad for a book and would mail in my check and eagerly await the material. Yes, if you were not an adult in the late 1980's – this was how it worked.

I ordered, by mail, my first set of runes and a basic book set and spent the winter learning the runes backwards and forwards. I was tally self-taught.

By the time the next summer came around, several of my friends felt that I should spend the summer at the Renaissance faire and do readings. That was just not the path I wanted to take but I did keep my interest in runes.

Over the years, I acquired a couple more sets and learned different spreads.

The idea for this workbook has been something I've thought about many times.

Many people do not have the time (or interest) to drive to a bookstore for a workshop. Runes require more than a couple hour workshop too.

In this day and age, unfortunately, the small metaphysical bookshops that I used to frequent are long gone. I drove an hour each way to two in the area when I found out about them.

The idea of a hands on workbook to learn the reading of runes and the meaning of each rune brewed in the back of my mind. After creating a Tarot Card learning workbook that I wrote to be personalized by the learner, I decided to take my idea of the runes learning workbook up a level. The first edition received a resounding yes based on the orders it received. This year, I decided to take a look at the original and make a few edits to bring readers an even better resource.

I created a workbook that contains the information and layout examples plus illustrations and exercises. Then tailored it around you – you'll work your way through the runes one by one. You'll do written exercises and your answers will be uniquely yours.

There are no right or wrong questions. You will work at your own pace.

You may have noticed that this book is traditional workbook sized – 8 ½ x 11. It was important to me to give you a professionally printed and bound workbook that was sturdy and also give you plenty of room to write.

I hope that you enjoy using and learning from this workbook as much as we have enjoyed creating it for you.

Finding the Perfect Set of Runes

You may already have a set of runes. I say have instead of own as I really don't know if runes are something we own or if they claim us, with the right ones coming on our path when the time is right.

I began with a basic set of stone runes. They were a perfect starting set. Mass produced – but they were still ideal, and I learned the basics using them over and over and over.

A couple years ago later, I crossed paths with a couple who made cool jewelry. He made a detailed set of runes from wood from me, one by one

A few years after that, a set etched on amethyst stones called my name and they also became a part of my collection.

Later in this book, we will discuss the color of runes and what the color can be associated with. While I find the color association to be of interest and useful, I will add – if a set calls to you, regardless of what color or material, then that set may be the one for you.

There are many places to find rune sets such as local shops. Your local indie bookstore may also stock them or be able to order a set for you. Don't be surprised as your familiarity with runes grows that other rune sets come across your path.

Elder Futhark Runes History

Let's travel back in time, way back - 2,000 plus years ago.

If you were living in Europe, chances are, you may have worked with runes or knew someone who did.

Runes are the mystical alphabet used by ancient European tribes 2,000 years ago to name places and things, attract luck and fortune, provide protection, and magically divine the course of future events.

Runes were usually carved onto stone or wood although in some cases bits of bones or leather hide may have been used depending upon where the rune caster dwelled.

The tools of the time such as the ax, knife, or chisel could not easily be used to form curved lines, so Runic letters were formed with straight lines only.

Virtually all of Europe used them at one time, but today they are best remembered for their use by the ancient Norse, The Vikings.

The oldest known form and arrangement of Runic letters, the Elder Futhark runes, are estimated by the British Museum to have been in use by the Vikings around 200 A.D.

Some believe it to be much earlier. In Norse, the Elder Futhark is read from right to left. "F U T H A R K" is the first 6 symbols of the Runic alphabet (note "th" is one letter).

The Runic alphabet is phonetic, each letter represents a sound, so double consonants are not used.

Words spelled with pp, dd, ll, etc. would be spelled using a single p, d, or l in Runes.

Quick Runes Reference Chart

Rune Symbol	Rune Name	Corresponding English Letter	Meaning	Uses	Element
ᚠ	Fehu	F	Wealth	Invites Wealth & Fulfillment of Goals	Fire
ᚢ	Uruz	U	Strength	Invites Creativity & Wealth	Earth
ᚦ	Thurisaz	TH	Force, Giant	Invites Strength for facing a Test, Difficulty or Powerful Enemy	Fire
ᚨ	Ansuz	A	God, Ancestor, Devine Breath	Invites Devine Power, Luck & Inspiration	Air
ᚱ	Raido	R	Journey, Wheel	Invites Renewal & Safe Journey - Physical or Spiritual	Air
ᚲ	Kenaz	K, C or Q	Torch, Fire, Light	Manifests Character & Personality	Fire
Blank Rune	Odin's Rune		Unlimited Potential	Unlimited Potential	

Rune Symbol	Rune Name	Corresponding English Letter	Meaning	Uses	Element
X	Gebo	G	Gift, Partnership	Invites Harmony, Joy & Generosity	Air
ᛈ	Wunjo	W or V	Glory, Joy, Perfection, Wish	Invites Glory & Wisdom	Earth
H	Hagalaz	H	Hail, Weapon of War	Carved Into Weapons of War	Ice
ᚾ	Nauthiz	N	Need, Necessity	Invites Destiny, To Accomplish the Impossible	Fire
I	Isa	I	Ice, Power	Invites Authority& Power; Symbol of Masculinity	Ice
ᛃ	Jera	Y or J	Year, Harvest	Invites Long Term Success & Luck; Gardener's Rune	Earth
ᛇ	Eihwaz	EI, AE	Yew Tree, Potential	Manifest Your Greatest Potential	Air
ᛈ	Pertho	P	Secrets, Chance	Invites Birth of New; Success in Games of Chance	Water
Y	Algiz	Z or X	Protection	Invites Protection, Health & Happiness	Air
Blank Rune	Odin's Rune		Unlimited Potential	Unlimited Potential	

Rune Symbol	Rune Name	Corresponding English Letter	Meaning	Uses	Element
S	Sowilo	S	Sun, Salvation	Invites Salvation, Spiritual Protection; Symbol of the Sun	Air
↑	Tiwaz	T	Creator, Spear, Tyr - The Norse God of Justice	Invites Strength of Purpose, Will Power & Resolution of Conflict	Air
B	Berkana	B	Birch Tree, Beloved	Invites Romance, Healing & Protection	Earth
ᛖ	Ehwaz	E	Horse, Friendship	Symbol of The Bonds of Friendship	Earth
M	Mannaz	M	Mankind, Knowledge	Invites Self Knowledge & Manifests True Self	Air
ᛚ	Laguz	L	Water, Lake	Invites Hope; Symbol of the Sustenance of Life	Water
ᛜ	Ingwauz	NG or ing	Fertility, True Love	Invites True Love, Friendship & Lasting Partnerships	Earth
Blank Rune	Odin's Rune		Unlimited Potential	Unlimited Potential	

Rune Symbol	Rune Name	Corresponding English Letter	Meaning	Uses	Element
ᛟ	Othala	O	Property, Homeland, Inheritance	Strengthens Family & Partnerships	Earth
ᛞ	Dagaz	D	Day, Good Luck	Good Luck Charm; Invites Spiritual Growth	Fire / Air
Blank Rune	Odin's Rune		Unlimited Potential	Unlimited Potential	

Merkstave - Runes Reversed Meanings

When runes are cast, one or more may not land right side up.

They may land upside down which is called Merkstave.

They can though, lay in opposition, which means that they can lay sideways or on their sides.

Casting a reversed rune itself is not necessarily negative, or a cause for concern or alarm.

Nine of the runes read the same, regardless of how you cast them.

The other fifteen runes can be read upright, in opposition or reversed.

Whether you draw your rune upright or reversed, it is always best to read both interpretations. Doing so will put you in touch with all aspects of the issue, including those not openly or currently being expressed.

The reversed reading interpretation draws attention to aspects of a situation that might impede movement or advancement. It may also indicate the fact that movement itself may be inappropriate at this time.

A reversed rune often signals the presence of an opportunity to challenge some aspect of your behavior, some area in your life which, until now, you have been unwilling to face.

Sometimes reversed meanings are a warning - but in a positive sense, like a blessing in disguise.

Detailed Rune Meaning, Description and Inverted Meaning

Following is information about each rune to give you detailed insight.

Merkstave as we covered above means a rune that is cast landed upside down.

In some cases, the upside down rune has a different meaning than if it had landed right side up.

You are absorbing an enormous amount of information as we go through this workbook. Do not expect to be able to immediately recall details of each rune.

You'll be reading and re-reading these descriptions and also, using them as a reference later.

You may find yourself more attuned to some runes and their meanings. Some may quickly feel like old friends, and some may take time and repetition – this is fully normal.

Rune 1 Literal Meanings of Fehu

ᚠ

Wealth, Cattle, Power

Fehu Description

The rune of Fehu symbolizes two branches which are growing off of a tree, or two horns of a cow. The literal meaning of Fehu is cattle, which in the past was a clear representation of a family's wealth.

Debts could be paid in cattle, and each man had a blood-price that could only be paid in cattle if they were killed unjustly.

Even if one did not tend and own his own cattle, part of the tribe's or clan's cattle was thought to belong to them depending on their status -- a bard, for example, was thought to have a blood-price almost equal to that of a king.

Cattle were both a measure of value, and a means of exchange -- much like money is used today.

How to Interpret Fehu

Wealth and success will soon arrive. Long hours of hard work which took place in the past which will soon be rewarded.

Wealth is always fluid and changing, but Fehu's appearance usually signifies an upswing in business affairs and earnings.

Carried with the rune Fehu is the warning to apply these new earnings to things that have solidity and permanence once they arrive. The fluidity of the earnings which are referenced here also reminds us that wealth slip easily through one's fingers.

Caution and restraint must be exercised.

Fehu also represents the attachment and sense of self-worth that one can obtain from wealth. It represents the dreams and goals that the individual has mapped out.

When Fehu turns up, these dreams may be coming close to realization.

Fehu also refers to the economics of relationships; not just debts in the financial sense of the term.

The appearance of this rune is an indication that there may be personal debts outstanding.

Was there a promise made that needs to be kept and has been long-standing?

If so, one should start down the road of making amends, as Fehu signifies that repayment must occur imminently.

Wealth is also power -- the rune frequently refers to power (and the exercise of power) that comes with success on the material plane.

Inverted Meaning of Fehu

The dark side of wealth is referenced here.

Inverted, Fehu's wealth is not lost, but the individual will likely experience the down-side of this wealth.

Money may corrupt, or friends may ask one for money and then deny their friendship when their requests are refused.

The appearance of the inverted Fehu serves as a reminder to manage one's own wealth and possessions effectively, rather than letting them assume control on their own.

Money, like power, can be used for both good and bad. It carries with it both positivity and negativity.

Fehu reversed is a reference to money's more negative aspects.

Rune 2 Literal Meanings of Uruz

ᚢ

Aurochs, Power

Description of Uruz

A mighty animal stands on four legs, two of which are obscured -- it raises its head to the sky.

The auroch was a massive (and now extinct) early European ox; their size was between a modern-day bison and a mammoth.

The Vikings prized these mighty creatures for their enormous horns, which they would use to drink out of.

In his Gallic Wars, Caesar wrote of the use of the aurochs hunt to initiate boys to manhood among the 'Germanii' (the Roman name for the German tribes).

This rune is also representative of the Norse God Ull.

Ull was the God of archery, hunting, and winter.

He is the leader of the hunt in Germanic folklore.

How to Interpret Uruz

This rune represents raw physical power.

It would not be uncommon for it to turn up in readings for an athlete, hunter, or a member of the military.

Uruz also represents sexuality and virility -- most commonly (but not exclusively) the male side of those attributes.

It may also represent a show of force which is unusually great for a specific individual. Its appearance often signals a significant internal life change if the individual involved in a rune reading is a man; or a shift in his masculine powers, depending on his age.

If the individual in a rune reading is female, it represents a man that is about to affect her life somehow, most likely in reference to a romantic or physical relationship.

It also refers to all of those aspects considered masculine that are still present in the female, such as athleticism, competitiveness, and more overt sexuality.

It may also refer to the abuse or overuse of those powers -- if the individual is an athlete, they may need to change their routine in order to avoid a sports injury.

Competitiveness may be getting in the way of advancement. Restraint may be suggested here.

Overall, Uruz refers to great strength, sexuality, athleticism, virility, and the employment of all of these things. It may also indicate that subtlety and inaction are both poor choices at this juncture.

Inverted Meaning of Uruz

A weakening of one's physical or emotional self.

Someone may be trying to use the individual's own power against them.

Watch out for energy-sapping situations and people; they are present when this rune is inverted.

Rune 3 Literal Meanings of Thurisaz

Thorn, Giant

Description of Thurisaz

In Norse mythology, the ancient and wicked Frost Giants bore an evil son named Loki whose sole mission in life was to torment mankind.

Although eternal enemies of the Norse gods, the Frost Giants consequently gave the Norse gods a purpose: the defense and protection of their sacred realms.

This rune represents the treachery of the Frost Giants and all the danger they represent, as well as the need for faithful vigilance and responsibility in the face of opposition.

Thurisaz is also called "the Thorn".

While the thorn is often seen as a source of pain, it can (as with the thorn of the rose) also be a source of profound beauty.

Contained in this rune is much of the old Norse view of winter and the elements: Beauty and danger combined in physical form. A time of trials.

How to Interpret Thurisaz

Thurisaz is the sacrifice that one must make in order to make progress in life.

It is the very essence of discipline. This rune references the pain that must be endured for the reward that lies at its end. It may be likened to a long period of study that lies before the start of a satisfying career.

A painful lesson learned.

Monetary hardship, a temporary separation, or anything that requires a personal sacrifice to "get through" to the other side of the situation.

Thursiaz represents harsh outside forces which stand in opposition -- particularly natural forces or forces on a larger scale.

On the positive side, Thurisaz also signifies discipline and the necessity of change: Things that are happening are meant to happen.

They are part of the grand cycle of life and nature. Those things that we are forced to endure will pave the way for good things in the future.

Inverted Meaning of Thurisaz

Being too resistant to change and not dealing with adversity.

Seeing only the short term of a situation, not the long term.

One should take care to understand the hardships that one is dealing with -- don't ignore them as they may become larger problems later.

Rune 4 Literal Meanings of Ansuz

Mouth, God

Description of Ansuz

Ansuz is the rune of Odin -- most powerful of all the gods in Norse mythology.

Odin is the All-Father and Norse god of wisdom.

Odin brought the wisdom of the runes to mankind through his self-sacrifice at the base of the World Tree.

Odin, much like Prometheus of Greek myth, has brought back something sacred and divine to the world of Man.

He takes an active interest in the affairs of Man and tries to guide humanity through their trials.

Ansuz is also, by virtue of being Odin's rune, a signifier of all forms of creativity, drawing, music, and fine arts.

How to Interpret Ansuz

Usually Ansuz signifies an authority figure in the life of the individual, such as an employer, teacher, or parent.

Whoever this figure may be, they are about to facilitate a positive life-changing event for the individual.

One may look forward to a promotion or bonus due to excellent work. A book may be written, a great work composed, a long-standing problem may be solved creatively.

Whatever this achievement is, assistance will be received from someone well qualified to give it.

Ansuz may also reference a highly creative person, or a creative solution to a long-standing problem.

Ansuz can also represent a spiritual teacher or leader, such as a priest, that will act as a guide for the individual on their spiritual and emotional journey.

To many, Ansuz is seen literally as the communication method of the word of the divine -- it is Odin's Stave, or wand. A message of guidance, creation and growth.

Inverted Meaning of Ansuz

The authority figures seemingly impede progress -- although this is likely only a perception. The appearance of this rune inverted suggests a resistance to genuine assistance.

Perhaps someone is not recognizing help when it is offered.

Don't bite the hand that feeds and guides.

There is wisdom in your immediate circle of contacts -- but first it must be invited and accepted.

Rune 5 Literal Meanings of Raidho

Riding, Journey, Wagon, Chariot

Description of Raidho

Raidho represents the overall life-path of a person.

The message of the rune of Raidho is that the stops along the way are less important here than the journey itself.

According to Norse mythology, the course of a life is determined by three weaving sisters called the Norns, who live at the base of the World Tree.

The three sisters weave the fates of all mankind. The first sister, Urdr ('becoming'), spins the yarn of each individual's fate. The second, Verdandi ('being'), measures the yarn. The third, Skuld ('that to come') cuts the yarn.

Like the three fates in Greek mythology, these sisters hold sway over the lives of all living things.

The Norns are also tasked with the tending of the roots of the World Tree with water from the well of Wyrd.

The rune Raidho reminds us that specific events are largely beyond our control.

Fate is not something that we can ever know or truly understand -- but something that must be respected, for it influences us from beyond our reach.

How to Interpret Raidho

In a reading, a physical journey is likely when Raidho appears.

This journey will likely be successful and will lead to a important changes in one's life. A move or a career change is foretold.

New experiences and insights await us over the horizon and will shape the course of our lives.

As with the lesson of the three Norns, the appearance of Raidho also suggests that all efforts to influence the situation (one way of the other) will likely fail.

The hands of fate are at work here -- fortunately the indication is largely positive. Raidho may also represent a change in lifestyle -- usually for the better.

At a literal level, Raidho may represent women, sisters or a career path.

Inverted Meaning of Raidho

Journeys may often just be detours off of one's primary path, not part of our primary life journey.

Moves and career changes can also mean disruptions in personal relationships, and these must be maintained in order to remain a whole person.

Failure to move on will cause stunted growth.

Rune 6 Literal Meanings of Kenaz

Torch, Ulcer

Description of Kenaz

Kenaz represents the brilliant flame of divine inspiration:

Rebirth through sacrifice -- Creation through fire.

This is the rune of the artisan, and often will frequently appear in readings for those engaged in artistic ventures or seeking creative solutions.

New ideas shine brightly in the darkness. What was once gloomy is now brilliantly lit by the introduction of creativity, light-giving energy and radiant warmth.

The torch of Kenaz represents illumination and an immense store of divine knowledge.

How to Interpret Kenaz

A solution to a long-standing issue.

Clarification will come after a long struggle -- the solution will seem simple after the long struggle that has led up to it.

Inspiration and the light of knowledge will pave the way for success in the current venture.

A sudden insight or enlightenment.

A moment is coming when someone will realize their purpose, their entire reason for being. Something (or someone) will light the way to this path.

Enlightenment and clarity do not come without sacrifice. There is often a price to pay for solutions and knowledge.

It will not be grievous, but it will require that the individual give something up that is precious to them. Knowledge, like the apple of the book of Genesis, may carry a steep cost.

Inverted Meaning of Kenaz

A flame is being darkened somewhere in the individual's life.

A source of inspiration is petering out. The individual should take care that they are not giving up on their dreams -- which could lead to a cooling of their life spark and spiritual suffering.

Do not be so quick to let go of a dream.

Rune 7 Literal Meanings of Gebo

ᚷ

Gift, Generosity, Wedding

Description of Gebo

The Rune of Gebo represents the act of giving in all it's forms.

The ancient Norse tale of "Brunhild" is a good one to illustrate the meaning of this rune: According to legend, the hero Sigurd fought and killed a mighty dragon and took a ring from its hoard.

Venturing onwards, he passed through a magical circle of fire where he found a sleeping warrior wearing shining armor.

He cut through the armor and revealed Brunhild, a beautiful Valkyrie (an angelic warrior woman of Valhalla) who had been kept there by Odin until a mortal man was brave enough to rescue her. Sigurd then gave her the ring and pledged his unending love to her.

Gebo represents a unification of two forces for the betterment of both parties.

Whether this is in a business deal or a romantic arrangement is of no consequence -- the result and meaning are the same.

Positive emotions, acts of selflessness and the giving of gifts are all referenced here. It should be noted that the legend of Brunhild also carries a somewhat sinister message: As legend has it -- the ring Sigurd gave to Brunhild had been cursed by the wicked god Loki.

The meaning here is that while intentions may be noble and emotions may be true -- the hand of fate must be respected: It is always present in all things.

How to Interpret Gebo

A gift will be given, or possibly a marriage proposal or an opportunity to put forward such a proposal is on its way.

A generous, bountiful person who wishes to enrich one's life, romantically or materially.

A divine gift, the gift of life or of balance. It is important that all parties remain equitable when the gift is given, or that balance which is so important to relationships may be endangered.

On another level, the rune of Gebo may represent sexual union.

Depending on the other runes that it appears with, it may mean a fleeting encounter; particularly if paired with Uruz.

This will be a very intense encounter and one that can be grown into something more if desired.

Inverted Meaning of Gebo

Gebo cannot be inverted.

Rune 8 Literal Meanings of Wunjo

Glory, bliss, joy

Description of Wunjo

A flag is planted in the field of battle after a resounding victory.

A long struggle has ended.

Victory gives way to days of song, celebration and rejoicing. According to Norse mythology, the great halls of Valhalla awaited all vanquished warriors and heroes after death -- as long as they had fought nobly and bravely in life.

What awaited the warriors in Valhalla was eternal glory, peace and joy: a state of eternal bliss.

Wunjo represents a spiritual ideal which cannot be maintained in the physical world.

The facets of Wunjo that we are able to experience in life are thought of as minor tastes of what was promised in Valhalla: a purity of pleasure and spiritual contentment.

How to Interpret Wunjo

Success and achievement of a goal.

The attainment of desire, possibly a person, a monetary desire, or otherwise.

Fantasies are soon to be fulfilled when this rune appears.

One must be careful that the desires in this rune do not give rise to an obsessive nature. Too much focus can be placed on the end goal rather than the means of achieving it.

The appearance of this rune may indicate a need to stop and reassess -- to take measure of the object of one's pursuits.

Wunjo reminds us that some fantasies are best left to the realm of fantasy.

Cautionary notes aside, Wunjo is a rune of great happiness and deserved celebration.

It is an indication to enjoy all that it has to offer.

Success and the true rewards of a job well done. Wunjo may also indicate a conflict that has not yet occurred -- but will prove beneficial -- and ultimately result in victory, joy and material gain.

Inverted Meaning of Wunjo

A goal takes longer to reach than was expected.

A journey towards a goal is painful.

The need to try harder in order to realize one's dreams.

There is a definite need to reassess the end goal and ensure that it is the right one when one sees Wunjo inverted.

Rune 9 Literal Meanings of Hagalaz

ᚺ

Hail

Description of Hagalaz

Ragnarok is the Norse version of Judgement Day, when it is foretold that the legendary Fenris wolf will devour the sun and plunge the world into darkness.

Our world and the world of the gods will both be destroyed by uncontrollable forces, and a vast process of universal rebirth will begin.

In a vastly smaller form, the destruction of Ragnarok is the kind of destruction one sees in the rune Hagalaz -- a destruction that is necessary in order to bring about rebirth of a new world, or a new phase of one's life.

How to Interpret Hagalaz

The appearance of Hagalaz is often an indication that we must let go of the past.

Only through the destruction of certain psychological aspects, emotional blocks, and ties to the past can we move forward.

While Hagalaz represents destruction, it also represents rebirth. That which currently exists may need to be destroyed in order for positive change to occur. Frequently it is a fear of destruction and loss which prevents future growth.

Hagalaz may also indicate that a temporary setback or obstacle has arisen -- one which the individual will necessarily get over very quickly.

Disappointment may also be indicated here, and a realization that the path that one has set out on is not the path that one is meant to be on.

Hagalaz reminds us that such disappointment is a necessary first-step in achieving change. A need to refocus and retask one's energies.

While the main lesson of this rune is positive, it must be cautioned that a setback will happen for a reason, and it is important not to let history repeat itself.

An opportunity will come in which one can better oneself. It may be painful, but ultimately it will prove beneficial.

Other possible literal meanings of Hagalaz in a reading include bad weather or emotional outbursts.

Inverted Meaning of Hagalaz

Cannot be inverted.

Rune 10 Literal Meanings of Nauthiz

$$\dagger$$

Need, necessity, trouble, constraint

Description of Nauthiz

A vast canyon or icy crevasse exists between one's current position and the position or goal that is desired. One needs to cross this great distance, but how?

Passage across this chasm must be secured or a shortage may become worse.

A need or shortfall is indicated here in all its forms: Nauthiz is the worker who has done a particular trade for years and finds themselves laid off, their trade obsolete.

Nauthiz is the harvest which falls short, unable to provide. Nauthiz is a yearning of the soul which is currently unfulfilled.

Nauthiz is a sudden demand which overwhelms one's stores and savings. Nauthiz indicates a time to retrain, relearn and plan effectively in order to get what is wanted from a particular situation.

Nauthiz is a rune of wanting, and it is generally a negative rune since it describes a lack of something.

If the reader believes the need referenced by Nauthiz is a constant need, then one's needs should be reevaluated.

If the need referenced by this rune is temporary in nature, it may be necessary to take steps to fill it.

In general, the rune Nauthiz represents a gap between that which one requires and the capacity that one has to fulfill that requirement.

How to Interpret Nauthiz

Something is desired or lacking by the querent.

Without fulfilling this need, forward motion will be difficult and unpleasant. Material need or sometimes impoverishment, whether real or imagined may also be described here.

The exact meaning of such impoverishment may be different for different people; for one person, poverty may mean one car in the family instead of two.

For another, it may mean no food for a week. Whatever the definition, the result is the same: a degradation of life-quality through a shortage of something.

Rectifying this situation will requires either diligence and intelligence in order to improve the situation.

A managing of one's desires may also be called for.

An alternate meaning of Nauthiz is a purely spiritual yearning for some greater level of enlightenment: a need created by spiritual impoverishment or a withering of the soul.

In some cases, Nauthiz represents a semi-permanent state of spiritual dissatisfaction, or one who is eternally dissatisfied despite material and emotional plenty.

It should be noted that while many see Nauthiz as a negative rune, depicting a shortage or a lack of something -- others see Nauthiz as a positive challenge -- a test that must be overcome to achieve the object of one's desire.

Inverted Meaning of Nauthiz

There are those who believe that Nauthiz cannot be reversed -- and others who say that it can.

With this particular rune, this decision must be made by the reader based upon the nature of the reading.

A possible inverted interpretation is as follows: The shortage is at its worst and the only way from here is up -- bear this in mind during the coming struggles.

Strong character is forged through difficult situations like this -- and fortunes made.

Some of the most successful and enduring people achieved greatness because they underwent extreme hardships at some point in their lives.

Rune 11 Literal Meaning of Isa

ᛁ

Ice

Description of Isa

This rune is one of the simplest of all.

Where Kenaz was fire, Isa represents the stillness and purity of ice. The elements of fire and ice are two of the most dominant in Norse mythology.

The Norse creation myth had the universe created out of the mating of these two materials.

Ice represents the ultimate stillness: A blanket of frozen immobility which seals the land, restricts travel and covers all that is life-giving and fertile.

Under its beautiful and concealing silence the rich earth below is nurtured and prepared for new energy and life.

Ice is representative of the feminine principle in Norse philosophy -- a stillness of contemplation and a preparation for new life: new hope and rebirth.

This is the Yang to the Yin of fiery Kenaz.

Without ice and winter to moisten the fields, the farming and harvest would be impossible. Where Kenaz is fire and aggression, Isa is meditative, still and ultimately a creative force.

How to Interpret Isa

A time of rest before action.

A period of meditation and recharging before action is continued.

It may be necessary to stop, take measure and look around in order to further assess a situation, rather to charge forward without direction.

When the ice thaws it will retreat from the land and one's direction will become clear. A time of fertile creation lies ahead.

While the pace of forward movement may seem slow and inhibited at this time, the seeds of rebirth are active beneath the surface.

The outward appearance of purity and stillness mask an explosion of fertility which lies ready in wait. All things will come in good time, and for now Isa reminds us that we must wait. The long winter is upon us now, but the cycle of seasons moves ever forward.

Also a path of reflection and meditation. Inner calmness must be maintained at this time in order for deeper reflection to occur.

Inverted Meaning of Isa

Isa cannot be inverted.

Rune 12 Literal Meanings of Jera

Summer, Plenty, Harvest

Description of Jera

Two scythes sweep in great arcs across endless fields of wheat, rye and flax.

The harvest has arrived, and with it a time of plenty and bounty.

The long hard winter has been endured, the hard work of tilling and planting has long since been completed, and now comes the time to reap the rewards for prior hardships. Life giving sustenance rises from the Earth.

Jera is an indication of plenty.

Because the rune refers to the harvest, it also indicates a time of subtle change.

The endless roll of seasons is referenced here and also the need to remember that leaner times may be on the horizon.

How to Interpret Jera

Jera represents change -- most frequently positive change.

This change is not the temporary reward of Wunjo, but a permanent reward after hardship, or series of hardships. Hard work is going to be rewarded.

Retirement, a sabbatical, or a vacation may be referenced here. Everything is happening as it should happen, and the time is coming to enjoy it.

Jera may also represent that little extra push that one needs to finish a job -- that final motivation that sees a job through to its successful conclusion.

As with a successful harvest, Jera is a rune of material gain.

It should be noted that Jera is a complementary rune to Gebo: if both runes turn up together, certain happiness in both relationships and money will occur.

Jera is often seen as a forward-looking rune which refers to an eventual positive resolution which will occur at some time in the future:

Often this pertains to legal resolutions.

Other possible literal meanings of Jera in a reading are a large, well-attended meal or outdoor festivities.

Inverted Meaning of Jera

Jera cannot be inverted.

Rune 13 Literal Meanings of Eihwaz

Yew Tree

Description of Eihwaz

The verdant Yew tree stands tall in a snowy field.

All around it is the still lifelessness of winter, yet the Yew remains supple and strong.

Yews are hardy trees which stay green even in winter.

Their red berries signify life in the harshest of environments -- a steadfast refusal to succumb to the opposition and hardship of the cold.

Yew trees have been linked to runes, the occult, and rites of passage in Europe since ancient Germanic times.

In Christianity, yew trees are often linked to immortality -- and are often planted in church yards expressly to signify this.

Historically, the wood of the yew tree also made the best bows, at one time a vital and sophisticated instrument of war -- used to kill the enemy at long range before they could draw close.

How to Interpret Eihwaz

A major and necessary life change may be about to take place; either the onset of adulthood, going away to college, marriage, retirement or a change in profession.

This change may seem full of uncertainty when it is first introduced, but it will become clear very quickly that such change is necessary.

A significant confrontation with one's inner fears and innermost insecurities may be at hand. While change is a constant process, the appearance of Eihwaz indicates an increase in the speed and intensity of change.

Change comes in many forms: mental, spiritual and physical. It is important to keep one's focus clear throughout the process: some change should be accepted as it is necessary and just. Other change may require a steadfast resolve and hardiness -- like the always green yew tree.

Through the trials of change come growth and spiritual expansion.

Resolve, flexibility and a focus on the importance of change will see one through the most difficult trials.

Eihwaz may also reference the need to address a problem well in advance, before it becomes serious.

Other possible literal meanings of Eihwaz in a reading are positive health, nature or the season of winter.

Inverted Meaning of Eihwaz

None. This rune cannot be inverted.

Rune 14 Literal Meanings of Perthro

Cup, Dice-Cup, Fate

Description of Perthro

This cup shape literally means a vessel -- possibly for casting lots.

This rune is one of the more controversial among runic scholars, as the "P" sound at the start does not actually appear anywhere else in early Germanic languages.

It is commonly thought that the rune's name, which is now lost to antiquity, was altered over the centuries with the development of more modern alphabets.

Perthro represents a vessel, something to be filled and drunk from. There is also significant evidence that the cup referenced by Perthro is a dice-cup, of the kind commonly used in games of chance and fate.

How to Interpret Pertho

The cup of Pertho represents fertility, mystery, and all things hidden.

The hand of fate, through Karma or divine predestination, is showing itself strongly in one's life.

While fate is often complex and impossible to understand, this rune indicates a powerful order and purpose behind seemingly random events.

Fate is both powerful and unknowable -- a force which we all must ultimately respect and give way to.

Intense forces of change that work behind the scenes are occurring at this time.

While these forces may be seen as positive or negative, the appearance of Pertho most commonly suggests positive forces -- unless of course it appears in a spread with a host of negative runes.

It should be noted that while we frequently view change as either "good" or "bad" -- Pertho reminds us that such black-and-white interpretation may represent an oversimplification of fate.

The change referenced by Pertho carries with it an infinite amount of complexity and subtlety.

To attempt to categorize change in simplistic terms of "positive" or "negative", is to attempt to understand fate itself: something no mortal can do.

When analyzing the meaning of Pertho, one should take care to remember that fate exists at a level that we can never truly know until such time that it is upon us.

What seems true may prove false, and vice versa. Only fate can tell.

Other possible literal meanings of Pertho in a reading are the act of drinking or games of chance.

Inverted Meaning of Pertho

There may be psychological issues present which the individual may need to explore further.

This may not represent a readiness to explore hidden mysteries further, but a burning desire that is not accompanied by the wisdom of experience.

Tread carefully, missteps are costly here.

Rune 15 Literal Meanings of Algiz

ᛦ

Defense, Protection, Sanctuary

Description of Algiz

The rune of Algiz depicts a person with arms upraised, elk's antlers, or a representation of the Norse God Heimdall who holds his sword in one hand and his horn in the other -- guarding the divine realm of Asgard.

In the old Germanic languages, Algiz means defense or protection.

Elhaz is another name for this rune, and it means elk. This refers to the four elks that feed off of the World Tree of Norse legend, or Yggdrasil.

The rune Algiz was commonly carved into the shields, swords and spears of warriors as a mark of protection and sanctuary from harm.

How to Interpret Algiz

As the best defense is often a good offense, this rune symbolizes protection in all of its forms; both offense and defense, proactive and reactive.

The appearance of this rune indicates the presence of a threat, and a need to guard against something.

Algiz signals that this protection may be expected from an outside source in a conflict that is either forthcoming or is already ongoing.

Algiz also refers to spiritual defenses and the act of drawing upon inner strength to actively protect our emotional well-being and our immediate surroundings.

Referenced here is our own internal system of checks and balances that makes up our conscience:

The soul reaching to the realm of the divine as an act of spiritual and physical protection. The more esoteric meanings of this complex rune aside, at its most basic level it symbolizes protection and helpful "brawn".

A threat is indicated, but the individual will come to no harm.

Inverted Meaning of Algiz

When inverted this rune is called Ihwar, meaning yew tree or yew bow.

The reversed position indicates that the situation may call for more of a defense than originally thought -- one's guard is down, the sword and horn are being held downwards rather than being held up to the sky.

Attacks must be anticipated, and defenses are down.

Rune 16 Literal Meanings of Sowilo

The sun.

Description of Sowilo

Sowilo, or the Sun Rune, symbolizes energy, life and fertility.

Warmth, positivity and drive flow from radiant Sowilo. Norse mythology describes the sun as a blazing disc which is pulled across sky in a chariot pulled by a great wolf.

One day, it is said, the wolf will stop pulling the chariot and eat the sun on the day of Ragnarok, the old Norse version of the judgement day.

While Sowilo indicates positive energy and success, Sowilo reminds us of the necessity to move on even after achieving that success.

Its action sustains itself and spurs the individual on to greater and more noble pursuits.

How to Interpret Sowilo

Success:

A more permanent and lifelong success than the harvest time of Jera.

Sowilo often refers to a dynamic, strong, steadfast, and charismatic personality. Energy, motivation, goodness, and all positive character attributes are referenced here.

A very successful outcome is indicated, perhaps more successful than one had predicted.

Sowilo is an extremely fortunate rune and is often considered the best possible rune in a reading. Sowilo represents an endless source of energy and brilliance: a renewal of hope and achievement. If a project or endeavor is beginning to seem to drag on Sowilo indicates a resurgence of positivity and progress.

Sowilo often references health issues and healing.

The sun's rays offer vital healing energy, and the appearance of this rune often indicates a positive resolution to a health issue, or a time of successful recovery.

Other possible literal meanings of Sowilo in a reading are: a reference to Summer or bright lights.

Inverted Meaning of Sowilo

Never with Sowilo

Rune 17 Literal Meanings of Tiwaz

$$\uparrow$$

Sound Leadership, Success in Battle, Personal Sacrifice

Description of Tiwaz

This rune references the legendary Norse warrior Tyr, who while struggling to save his people, lost his hand to a giant wolf named Fenris.

While Tyr was victorious and showed incredible resolve and bravery -- his victory came at great personal cost. Tyr's victory ensured the safety of his fellow clan, but through the sacrifice of his victory, he rendered himself useless in his chosen trade.

Tiwaz is a positive rune, but it carries a stern message of responsibility, cost and loyalty.

How to Interpret Tiwaz

Ultimately, this is an extremely positive rune signifying victory in battle and success in competition.

Direct action and powerful forward motion is indicated. Sound leadership is often characterized by selflessness.

A good leader places his people and his clan before his own needs. Management and leadership skills are referenced positively here.

From a spiritual perspective, Tiwaz represents a spiritual breakthrough that awakens new levels of understanding. It should be noted, that as with the warrior Tyr, the success indicated by this rune often carries a painful price.

It can literally foretell a minor injury, and may indicate a personal loss (or injury) accompanied by a great gain one's family, company or team.

The appearance of Tiwaz generally means that the proper direction of this force, usually in business, will net the individual a victory through proper application of force and pressure.

Inverted Meaning of Tiwaz

Progress through aggression may not be the answer in this particular situation.

Find another way of achieving the desired outcome.

Application of too much force will drive success away.

Rune 18 Literal Meanings of Berkana

Birch tree.

Description of Berkana

The birch tree was a symbol of fertility in quite a few different myths from European folklore.

Likewise, the shape of this rune implies a stylized female form.

Berkana (also "Berkano") represents the universal idea of the Goddess and the powerful bond between mother and child.

A powerful sense of nurturing, protection, support and creation are indicated by this rune.

All of the feminine mysteries are contained in Berkana, as the traditionally male mysteries are contained in Uruz.

As with Uruz, the gender-leaning of the rune does not necessarily mean that the rune applies strictly to a male or a female person -- and can also apply to a nurturing, supportive male.

How to Interpret Berkana

Either a pregnancy or a new start in a person's life is indicated here -- or the fertility of a new business venture.

Berkana indicates a fresh perspective, a good start.

Aside from a physical birth, a rebirth, or a burst of creativity may be indicated.

Berkana frequently refers to domestic issues and personal relationships -- particularly those involving emotional support, nurturing and "standing by" loved ones.

Berkana can also represent a person who is a healer, whether a nurse, doctor, or other kind of medical practitioner.

The energies of this rune are healing and life-giving.

Inverted Meaning of Berkana

Growth is being stunted through a stubborn refusal to channel creative and healing forces.

Learn to accept the rites of passage of life -- don't ignore them or they will just cause you more pain than necessary.

Berkana inverted, can also signify friction within relationships -- or even betrayal.

Rune 19 Literal Meanings of Ehwaz

ᛗ

Two Horses, Travel

Description of Ehwaz

While one horse frequently symbolizes the warrior, two horses (as are used to pull carts) symbolize travel and progress.

The rune Ehwaz represents journeys, distant places and events which have not yet transpired. In rune lore, Ehwaz is also regarded as being a depiction of Sleipnir, the Norse god Odin's eight-legged horse -- which symbolizes fluidity and smoothness of motion.

Ehwaz, encompasses energy, force, and direct (although not necessarily swift) motion. Like any horse, this progress must be carefully managed and tended, in order for its full potential to be realized.

How to Interpret Ehwaz

Most simply put, Ehwaz symbolizes forward energy and movement.

Ehwaz may represent general travel and steady progress-- or it may literally represent a car, plane or another method of transportation.

Ehwaz also symbolizes communication over long distances and can refer to an important message that one will give or receive.

Harmonious concord and pulling together as a team is also referenced here.

When Ehwaz appears in a spread, it empowers the runes around it and augments their meanings simply by virtue of its directional energy and forward movement.

Teamwork, forward-motion, communication, and consistent drive will win the day when this rune turns up.

Inverted Meaning of Ehwaz

Blocked movement.

An inability to act.

The best solution at this point may be passivity, not action.

A failure to communicate or act in unison.

Rune 20 Literal Meanings of Mannaz

Man, Humankind

Description of Mannaz

Mannaz symbolizes all of humanity, joined together for the purposes of attaining a common goal.

On a more personal scale, Mannaz may represent our circle of family and friends -- and the common goals which unite us.

An intertwining of man and woman is also referenced here, and a combining of their souls into a single entity.

On a philosophical level -- Mannaz reminds us that we are one.

All purposes and goals ultimately flow into a greater purpose which is shared by all mankind.

How to Interpret Mannaz

Mannaz represents a group of people, most frequently the community immediately surrounding the individual -- and often references the ways in which that group perceives the individual in question.

Friends are being made and a community is being formed and served. The individual is giving a part of themselves up for the greater good.

If a reading deals with great tasks, the appearance of Mannaz often indicates that assistance will come from others.

This rune may also refer to a spiritual community, such as that of a church or a religious group of some kind; the individual may be interacting with this new community soon.

The appearance of Mannaz frequently signifies the intensification and betterment of the person's relationships with people and community.

This often refers just to social relationships, rather than business or romantic relationships. The appearance of this rune suggests that the important factor may not necessarily be the individual doing the reading, but the people in his or her immediate sphere of contacts.

While many runes deal with the individual, Mannaz is a reminder to step back and consider a larger group -- the family or community.

Mannaz also directly relates to an individual's place within a community, how he or she performs, and how he or she is perceived.

Inverted Meaning of Mannaz

One must make peace with oneself before turning outward to focus on friends or community.

Often we will seek community to heal a problem within ourselves that cannot be fixed from an outward source -- meditation and constructive self-reflection is required.

Rune 21 Literal Meanings of Laguz

Ocean, sea, water

Description of Laguz

Like a wave waiting to carry a Viking ship to a distant shore, Laguz represents the endless possibilities and the nourishment of water.

To the Norse, Laguz also represented the wild forces of the ocean, which if not respected could lead to destruction and death. Laguz speaks to our primal fears and insecurities -- that ultimately we are small and insignificant in the face of opposition, and that should everything go wrong, we may be powerless to help ourselves. The ocean, like so many images in Norse lore -- is another highly complex and mixed image: it contains secrets, treasures, promises and dangers. The ocean represents life, death and a vastness of scale which reminds us of our individual insignificance. The ocean is a strongly female force.

The appearance of Laguz in a reading will frequently indicate a woman (either the querent if she is female, or if the querent is male: the most important woman in his life).

Laguz also represents the moon and the cycle of the ocean's tides.

How to Interpret Laguz

Laguz is typically a negative rune. It signifies uncertainty, and a powerlessness to act in the face of overwhelming opposition.

If however, the question being asked is "Should I continue" with something, Laguz instructs very clearly to continue in the same way that water flows uninterrupted.

The appearance of Laguz suggests that something that has previously been hidden will be revealed.

What was hidden may not be a pleasant thing to witness, but it will be necessary. This may allude to something like a treacherous spouse or a thieving employee -- unpleasant but necessary for the individual to uncover.

Frequently this rune references how other people feel about the someone.

Perception is indicated here. ie: It is necessary to uncover what is hidden in a person's life in order for them to move forward.

Other possible literal meanings of Laguz in a reading are: A woman (either the querent or a woman significant to the querent), the ocean or beach, social opposition.

Inverted Meaning of Laguz

An obstinate need to ignore that which is hidden and needs to be uncovered.

The rune Laguz may turn up inverted when a spouse knows that their partner is cheating,but is doing nothing about it to maintain the status quo.

The appearance of this rune inverted means that the status quo is not worth maintaining and they should remove themselves from the situation as soon as possible.

Rune 22 Literal Meanings of Ingwaz

The Earth, Agriculture, Nature, Ing.

Description of Ingwaz

Ing is one of the alternate names for Freyr, Norse god of agriculture.

Legend says that Freyr travelled around the Earth in a chariot, dispensing fertility and happiness to his people.

How to Interpret Ingwaz

Ingwaz symbolizes the Earth and our deep relation to it.

Its appearance may mean that we need to spend more time in nature or pay more attention to the natural order of things.

Outdoor activities are referenced here, including sports, hiking and the ocean.

The appearance of Ingwaz may also indicate a need to pay attention to one's body, either through the addition of an exercise regimen to one's life or a change in diet.

A healthy metabolism and lifestyle are indicated here -- and may suggest a need to focus on a sound body in order to achieve a sound mind.

This is also a rune of growth: representing the actual act of growth rather than the rewards that await one at the end of the cycle.

Personal growth may occur through some event in the near future.

On a grander level, Ingwaz can represent the wholeness of the Earth or of humanity.

Overall human conditions, or global issues.

At a smaller scale, the appearance of Ingwaz may represent food or a meal with friends.

Inverted Meaning of Ingwaz

None. This rune cannot be inverted.

Rune 23 Literal Meanings of Dagaz

ᛞ

Dawn, Day

Description of Dagaz

Dagaz references the most basic of all cycles: Night and Day.

This powerful rune is a reminder of the cyclical nature of all things.

What rises must fall. What increases must decrease.

All things are interconnected and in a state of constant flux.

Dagaz is the rune of awakening -- new worlds, new possibilities and new opportunities arise as others fade away.

Day and night are (and will always be) in perfect proportion.

There is balance in all things, celestial and material. Night has passed and a new day is beginning.

How to Interpret Dagaz

This very positive rune signifies a well-led life, an individual who is happy with themselves and their position in life.

Balance has been achieved. Positive, good forces will be at work very shortly, because expectations have been managed and risks properly assessed.

Balance and harmony reign supreme -- events will soon take a turn for the better. One has already crossed through a place of darkness and now, a new day dawns.

A major transformation either spiritual or material, is occurring as the first light of a new day breaks over the horizon.

Possibilities are everywhere. If some rare cases, if success in a matter has been at hand for a long period of time, Dagaz may indicate a change to that cycle -- a new day which brings with it fundamental shift to underlying expectations.

More literal references here can also be to a time of day (the early morning), and to new business endeavors, new relationships and new pursuits.

Inverted Meaning of Dagaz

May not be inverted

Rune 24 Literal Meanings of Othala

ᛟ

Property, Estate, A House, Land

Description of Othala

Othala is the rune of the ancient clan lands:

Historic land and property which has a strong spiritual connection to the individual.

Othala is the crowning achievement which lies at the end of the runic journey.

It is the last rune, if one reads them in sequence.

These ancestral lands are the result of a life of successful spiritual pursuit and hard work. Othala is that physical manifestation of everything that has been earned by previous generations and by this one: particularly, (but not limited to) a house or property.

Othala represents our home: our lands, our community, our nation, our identity, our personal assets and the assets of our friends and family.

Othala is a physical representation of both our past and our destiny -- a reminder of who we are, and a symbol of the greatness we aspire to.

The noble rune, Othala references both responsibility and pride, history and future, honor and hard work.

It is a reminder both of our ancestry and the material legacy we will leave behind.

Othala is a reminder that there is greatness in small things -- What we do here will survive us.

What was done in the past is all around us now and should be respected.

How to Interpret Othala

The security and safety that comes with material wealth is referenced here: Richness in the sense of home and family, as well as material wealth.

A favorable situation will give the individual greater security very shortly -- but hard work will always be required to maintain the fruits of this situation.

Othala may represent an individual who has overcome many obstacles and has now come home to put their feet up and enjoy their lives as they deserve to.

This individual has come to a place in their lives where they have found success -- it is now time for them to recognize the importance of home and family and enjoy the fruits of both.

Wealth, property, and land are all considerations when this rune turns up, and all in a positive fashion.

Alternatively, Othala may represent an ancestral land, or the country of one's forebears. Inheritance and history are powerfully referenced here.

Inverted Meaning of Othala

Inability to accept family as a source of happiness in one's life.

Chaos on the home front.

Poverty and loss of land and/or wealth.

RUNE MEANINGS WORKBOOK SECTION

Get your pencils sharpened as we will be soon beginning the exercise section of this book.

We will walk through each rune symbol one by one.

There are no right or wrong answers -you'll learn the sign, name, phoneme (sound), and short description of the meaning of each of the twenty-four runes that comprise the Elder Futhark.

To make each rune come to life, we will go over a few questions based on your life experiences to help you connect with each rune and the meaning of it.

RUNE 1 Fehu

ᚠ

Name: Fehu, cattle. Phoneme: F.
Meaning: wealth.

In the beginning days of rune casting, wealth was equated to how many cattle own owned hence the word Fehu being this rune's name.

While we usually think of wealth as how much money one has, objects and also matters such as health or landing a good paying job may be a goal to equal wealth for some. For example, getting a ½ carat diamond ring may make one feel wealthy or paying off a car loan.

Name some examples of what makes you feel wealthy.

____

____

____

____

____

____

____

____

____

____

____

____

RUNE 2 Uruz

ᚢ

Name: Uruz, aurochs. Phoneme: U (long and/or short).
Meaning: strength of will.

Strength of will is often what gets us through the darkest days. It can be what makes us not give up when being on a diet is incredibly hard or when learning a new subject.

Write examples of when you have used your strength of will.

RUNE 3 Thurisaz

$$\Þ$$

Name: Thurisaz, Giant Phoneme: Th (both soft and hard).
Meaning: danger, suffering.

Danger and suffering may have played a larger role 2000 years ago but we still endure it today.

When I was a child, I was crossing a busy street holding my mother's hand. I saw a shiny penny in a crack of pavement, pulled loose to grab it and was very nearly struck by a car. Many years later, that moment still comes to mind when I think of the word "danger". Danger can be even the most minute of moments – but it instantly reminds you of that fight or flight moment.

Write examples of when you were in danger and when you had experienced suffering

RUNE 4 Ansuz

Name: Ansuz, an Aesir god. Phoneme: A (long and/or short).
Meaning: prosperity, vitality.

Prosperity is not necessarily a monetary situation, but in some cases it is – it all depends on your unique situation.

What time period in your life comes to mind when you think prosperity and vitality? Write the details below.

RUNE 5 Raidho

ᚱ

Name: Raidho, journey on horseback. Phoneme: R.
Meaning: movement, work, growth.

Movement often signifies growth, even if we do not realize it at the time. Think of a time when you took action and the growth that occurred (it may have been physical, mental, spiritual, monetary or something else).

Write the details below.

RUNE 6 Kenaz

〈

Name: Kenaz, ulcer. Phoneme: K.
Meaning: mortality, pain.

In life, we all face the moment when we recognize mortality. It may be as a child when a pet or grandparent dies or later in life. What comes to mind when you think back to when you first really thought about mortality?

Write your recollection below.

____

____

____

____

____

____

____

____

____

____

____

____

____

____

____

____

____

RUNE 7 Gebo

Χ

Name: Gebo, gift. Phoneme: G.
Meaning: generosity.

Generosity is a wonderful thing. It may be a gesture, a simple act such as sharing a piece of candy or a larger act such as helping someone down on their luck.

Think about when you accepted a gift of generosity and also when your generosity helped another.

Write down both of these recollections below.

RUNE 8 Wunjo

ᚹ

Name: Wunjo, joy Phoneme: W.
Meaning: joy, ecstasy.

Sometimes, moments of joy stay with us forever.

It may be a simple thing that caused much joy, such as riding a pony on a sunny summer day or the birth of a child – the moment of experiencing joy, that memory may stay with us our entire life, no matter how fleeting it was at the time.

Recall that moment in your life and write the details below.

RUNE 9 Hagalaz
ᚺ

Name:Hagalaz, hail. Phoneme: H.
Meaning: destruction, chaos.

Hagalaz brings us destruction and chaos.

Life changing events that come into our lives, sometimes coming in abruptly and leaving just as abruptly, leaving us reeling.

Think about a time that destruction and chaos came calling. How did you feel? How did you react? What was the aftermath?

Share your thoughts on the situation below.

RUNE 10 Nauthiz

†

Name: Nauthiz, need. Phoneme: N.
Meaning: need, unfulfilled desire.

Having an unfilled desire is something that may gnaw on you in the wee hours of the night or a moment that fleetingly crosses your mind.

It may be a small matter that you kick yourself for not doing or something much larger that haunts you.

Think of something that as a child or even now, was an unfulfilled desire.

Did you take action on the matter?

Why or why not? If so, was the outcome what you expected? Write your thoughts on the matter below.

____

____

____

____

____

____

____

____

____

____

____

____

____

____

RUNE 11 Isa

Ι

Name: Isa, ice. Phoneme: I (long and/or short).
Meaning: Authority and power

Think back to a time when you felt you had no authority or power over a matter. Then think about a time when you did have authority and power (it may be the same type of situation or not – either way is okay). Write down the two examples below.

RUNE 12 Jera

Name: Jera, year. Phoneme: Germanic J, modern English Y.
Meaning: harvest, reward.

There may be nothing better than harvesting the end result of something we have tended to, sometimes for years. Maybe a new business, paying off a debt, completing education on a topic, receiving a bonus for a job well done, investing in stocks, growing a bountiful garden or even finishing your taxes only to find your refund is larger than expected.

Think of a time when you reaped a wonderful harvest and how good it made you feel. Write the details below.

RUNE 13 Eihwaz

ᛇ

Strength and stability are traits we often value and admire.

Having someone to lean on who shows us strength and stability often gives us strength and helps calm the storm that may be raging within.

Being the person someone else can depend on is a wonderful accomplishment and often a special calling.

Think about a time you were someone's strength and stability and also a time when someone gave you strength and stability. Write the details below.

RUNE 14 Pertho

Name: Pertho Phoneme: P.
Meaning: The cup of Pertho represents fertility, mystery, and all things
hidden. The hand of Fate, through Karma or divine predestination, is
showing itself strongly in one's life.

Have you ever felt that the hand of Fate played a role in your life or someone you know? Write the details below.

____

____

____

____

____

____

____

____

____

____

____

____

____

RUNE 15 Algiz

ᛉ

Name: Algiz Phoneme: Z.
Meaning: protection from enemies, defense of that which one loves.

Recall a time that you have had protection from enemies or protected someone from an enemy. It may have been a grade school bully or something else. What came to mind when you read the meaning of Algiz? Write the details below.

____

____

____

____

____

____

____

____

____

____

____

____

____

____

____

RUNE 16 Sowilo

S

Name: Sowilo, sun. Phoneme: S.
Meaning: success, solace.

We've all had our moment in the sun, our time to shine – it may have been winning a classroom spelling bee, or making the honor roll or an accomplishment later in life. Write the details of what came to mind when you thought about a success you have had.

____

____

____

____

____

____

____

____

____

____

____

____

____

____

RUNE 17 Tiwaz

↑

Name: Tiwaz, the god Tiwaz. Phoneme: T.
Meaning: victory, honor.

Victory is a wonderful feeling, especially when there is honor in the way it was accomplished.
Think of a time when you achieved victory and write the details below.

____

____

____

____

____

____

____

____

____

____

____

____

____

____

____

RUNE 18 Berkana

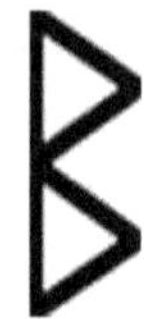

Name: Berkana, birch. Phoneme: B.
Meaning: fertility, growth, sustenance.

Accomplishing something that helps you grow, either in education, your personal life, business or life in general is often a very fulfilling feeling. That moment often is the seed of a new beginning. Think of a time you experienced growth and your hopes of what was to come. Write the details below.

RUNE 19 Ehwaz

ᛗ

Name: Ehwaz, horse.Phoneme: E (long and/or short).
Meaning: trust, faith, companionship.

Trust, faith and companionship are important in our lives just as they were 2,000 years ago when the runes began being used. When you think of trust, faith, companionship, what event in your life comes to mind? Write the details below.

RUNE 20 Mannaz

ᛗ

Name: Mannaz, man. Phoneme: M.
Meaning: support.

Supporting someone or being supported is often a life saving moment. Sometimes it is a monetary type of support and sometimes it is just a nod that shows you are behind someone.

Think of a time someone supported you and also a time you supported someone. Write down what comes to mind below.

RUNE 21 Laguz

Name: Laguz. Phoneme: L.
Meaning: formlessness, chaos, potentiality, the unknown.

While chaos can be unsettling, it also can have potential to opening formerly unthought of or pathways that previously unknown.

Recall a time when chaos opened the door to something good. Write the details below.

RUNE 22 Ingwaz

Name: Ingwaz, the god Ingwaz. Phoneme: Ng.
Meaning: fertilization, the beginning of something, the actualization of potential.

The moment when you see the potential of something unfolding into something amazing, is truly a golden moment. Recall a time when this occurred in your life and write the details below.

____

____

____

____

____

____

____

____

____

____

____

____

____

____

RUNE 23 Othala

⬦

Name: Othala, inheritance. Phoneme: O (long and/or short).
Meaning: inheritance, heritage, tradition, nobility.

An inheritance may be monetary but it also may be a legacy, handed down as a tradition, over the years. Do you have traditions in your family that began generations ago by another family member and/or have you started a tradition yourself? Write down the details below.

RUNE 24 Dagaz

ᛞ

Name: Dagaz, day. Phoneme: D.
Meaning: hope, happiness.

Having hope and happiness in your life makes things seem better and brighter. Sometimes even the smallest of things can bring great happiness.

What memory comes to mind when you think of a memory of happiness? Write down the details below.

Congratulations!

You have completed the largest exercise in this workbook. I hope you feel that you have truly accomplished a big step as you have definitely done so.

We have more exercises to cover but first, take a moment to congratulate yourself and write down how it makes you feel to have completed this exercise.

The next two exercises were created to help you increase your familiarity with each rune.

Exercise 2

In this exercise, you are going to pull runes out of your rune bag one by one and match them to this sheet. I have included several copies of this exercise for future practice.

This exercise was created to help you become more comfortable in quickly recognizing the name of each rune.

Rune Symbol	Rune Name	Matched:
ᚠ	Fehu	
ᚢ	Uruz	
ᚦ	Thurisaz	
ᚨ	Ansuz	
ᚱ	Raido	
ᚲ	Kenaz	
ᚷ	Gebo	
ᚹ	Wunjo	
ᚺ	Hagalaz	
ᚾ	Nauthiz	
ᛁ	Isa	
ᛃ	Jera	
ᛇ	Eihwaz	
ᛈ	Pertho	
ᛉ	Algiz	
ᛋ	Sowilo	
ᛏ	Tiwaz	
ᛒ	Berkana	
ᛖ	Ehwaz	
ᛗ	Mannaz	
ᛚ	Laguz	
ᛜ	Ingwauz	
ᛟ	Othala	
ᛞ	Dagaz	
Blank Rune	Odin's Rune	

Rune Symbol	Rune Name	Matched:
ᚠ	Fehu	
ᚢ	Uruz	
ᚦ	Thurisaz	
ᚨ	Ansuz	
ᚱ	Raido	
ᚲ	Kenaz	
ᚷ	Gebo	
ᚹ	Wunjo	
ᚺ	Hagalaz	
ᚾ	Nauthiz	
ᛁ	Isa	
ᛃ	Jera	
ᛇ	Eihwaz	
ᛈ	Pertho	
ᛉ	Algiz	
ᛊ	Sowilo	
ᛏ	Tiwaz	
ᛒ	Berkana	
ᛖ	Ehwaz	
ᛗ	Mannaz	
ᛚ	Laguz	
ᛜ	Ingwauz	
ᛟ	Othala	
ᛞ	Dagaz	
Blank Rune	Odin's Rune	

Rune Symbol	Rune Name	Matched:
ᚠ	Fehu	
ᚢ	Uruz	
ᚦ	Thurisaz	
ᚨ	Ansuz	
ᚱ	Raido	
ᚲ	Kenaz	
ᚷ	Gebo	
ᚹ	Wunjo	
ᚺ	Hagalaz	
ᚾ	Nauthiz	
ᛁ	Isa	
ᛃ	Jera	
ᛇ	Eihwaz	
ᛈ	Pertho	
ᛉ	Algiz	
ᛊ	Sowilo	
ᛏ	Tiwaz	
ᛒ	Berkana	
ᛖ	Ehwaz	
ᛗ	Mannaz	
ᛚ	Laguz	
ᛜ	Ingwauz	
ᛟ	Othala	
ᛞ	Dagaz	
Blank Rune	Odin's Rune	

Rune Symbol	Rune Name	Matched:
ᚠ	Fehu	
ᚢ	Uruz	
ᚦ	Thurisaz	
ᚨ	Ansuz	
ᚱ	Raido	
ᚲ	Kenaz	
ᚷ	Gebo	
ᚹ	Wunjo	
ᚺ	Hagalaz	
ᚾ	Nauthiz	
ᛁ	Isa	
ᛃ	Jera	
ᛇ	Eihwaz	
ᛈ	Pertho	
ᛉ	Algiz	
ᛊ	Sowilo	
ᛏ	Tiwaz	
ᛒ	Berkana	
ᛖ	Ehwaz	
ᛗ	Mannaz	
ᛚ	Laguz	
ᛜ	Ingwauz	
ᛟ	Othala	
ᛞ	Dagaz	
Blank Rune	Odin's Rune	

Rune Symbol	Rune Name	Matched:
ᚠ	Fehu	
ᚢ	Uruz	
ᚦ	Thurisaz	
ᚨ	Ansuz	
ᚱ	Raido	
ᚲ	Kenaz	
ᚷ	Gebo	
ᚹ	Wunjo	
ᚺ	Hagalaz	
ᚾ	Nauthiz	
ᛁ	Isa	
ᛃ	Jera	
ᛇ	Eihwaz	
ᛈ	Pertho	
ᛉ	Algiz	
ᛋ	Sowilo	
ᛏ	Tiwaz	
ᛒ	Berkana	
ᛖ	Ehwaz	
ᛗ	Mannaz	
ᛚ	Laguz	
ᛜ	Ingwauz	
ᛟ	Othala	
ᛞ	Dagaz	
Blank Rune	Odin's Rune	

Exercise 3

In this exercise, you'll pull a rune, find the symbol on the sheet and write the name next to it.

As with the above exercise, you will have several copies of this exercise for practice.

Being able to quickly recognize the rune and recall the name is not something that happens immediately for most people who are learning the runes. Everyone learns at their own speed.

Rune Symbol	Rune Name	Matched:
ᚠ		
ᚢ		
ᚦ		
ᚨ		
ᚱ		
ᚲ		
ᚷ		
ᚹ		
ᚺ		
ᚾ		
ᛁ		
ᛃ		
ᛇ		
ᛈ		
ᛉ		
ᛊ		
ᛏ		
ᛒ		
ᛖ		
ᛗ		
ᛚ		
ᛟ		
ᛞ		
ᛝ		
Blank Rune		

Rune Symbol	Rune Name	Matched:
ᚠ		
ᚢ		
ᚦ		
ᚨ		
ᚱ		
ᚲ		
ᚷ		
ᚹ		
ᚺ		
ᚾ		
ᛁ		
ᛃ		
ᛇ		
ᛈ		
ᛉ		
ᛊ		
ᛏ		
ᛒ		
ᛖ		
ᛗ		
ᛚ		
ᛜ		
ᛟ		
ᛞ		
Blank Rune		

Rune Symbol	Rune Name	Matched:
ᚠ		
ᚢ		
ᚦ		
ᚨ		
ᚱ		
ᚲ		
ᚷ		
ᚹ		
ᚺ		
ᚾ		
ᛁ		
ᛃ		
ᛇ		
ᛈ		
ᛉ		
ᛊ		
ᛏ		
ᛒ		
ᛖ		
ᛗ		
ᛚ		
ᛜ		
ᛟ		
ᛞ		
Blank Rune		

Rune Symbol	Rune Name	Matched:
ᚠ		
ᚢ		
ᚦ		
ᚨ		
ᚱ		
ᚲ		
ᚷ		
ᚹ		
ᚺ		
ᚾ		
ᛁ		
ᛃ		
ᛇ		
ᛈ		
ᛉ		
ᛊ		
ᛏ		
ᛒ		
ᛖ		
ᛗ		
ᛚ		
ᛜ		
ᛞ		
ᛟ		
Blank Rune		

Rune Symbol	Rune Name	Matched:
ᚠ		
ᚢ		
ᚦ		
ᚨ		
ᚱ		
ᚲ		
ᚷ		
ᚹ		
ᚺ		
ᚾ		
ᛁ		
ᛃ		
ᛇ		
ᛈ		
ᛉ		
ᛋ		
ᛏ		
ᛒ		
ᛖ		
ᛗ		
ᛚ		
ᛜ		
ᛟ		
ᛞ		
Blank Rune		

Rune Symbol	Rune Name	Matched:
ᚠ		
ᚢ		
ᚦ		
ᚨ		
ᚱ		
ᚲ		
ᚷ		
ᚹ		
ᚺ		
ᚾ		
ᛁ		
ᛃ		
ᛇ		
ᛈ		
ᛉ		
ᛋ		
ᛏ		
ᛒ		
ᛖ		
ᛗ		
ᛚ		
ᛜ		
ᛞ		
ᛟ		
Blank Rune		

Rune Symbol	Rune Name	Matched:
ᚠ		
ᚢ		
ᚦ		
ᚨ		
ᚱ		
ᚲ		
ᚷ		
ᚹ		
ᚺ		
ᚾ		
ᛁ		
ᛃ		
ᛇ		
ᛈ		
ᛉ		
ᛋ		
ᛏ		
ᛒ		
ᛖ		
ᛗ		
ᛚ		
ᛝ		
ᛞ		
Blank Rune		

Rune Symbol	Rune Name	Matched:
ᚠ		
ᚢ		
ᚦ		
ᚨ		
ᚱ		
ᚲ		
ᚷ		
ᚹ		
ᚺ		
ᚾ		
ᛁ		
ᛃ		
ᛇ		
ᛈ		
ᛉ		
ᛋ		
ᛏ		
ᛒ		
ᛖ		
ᛗ		
ᛚ		
ᛜ		
ᛟ		
ᛞ		
Blank Rune		

Rune Symbol	Rune Name	Matched:
ᚠ		
ᚢ		
ᚦ		
ᚨ		
ᚱ		
ᚲ		
ᚷ		
ᚹ		
ᚺ		
ᚾ		
ᛁ		
ᛃ		
ᛇ		
ᛈ		
ᛉ		
ᛊ		
ᛏ		
ᛒ		
ᛖ		
ᛗ		
ᛚ		
ᛜ		
ᛞ		
ᛟ		
Blank Rune		

Rune Spreads Introduction

The first step in learning to read the runes must be to get to know the runes themselves.

This doesn't necessarily mean memorizing interpretations out of a book, although the literal meanings of the rune names should be memorized as a starting point.

At this point, you should have some familiarity with the runes if you have read this workbook in order and done the exercises.

Next we will go over several different Rune Spreads.

I know it is tempting to just jumping to this section, but it is truly for your own benefit to follow each part of this workbook in order.

Keeping a Rune Readings Journal

Always keep a record of your rune readings in a journal.

You may use any type of journal or notebook. From one at the dollar store to a higher priced leather bound book – the choice is yours.

The main thing is, making this journal only for your runes.

When you begin using your journal, record which runes landed face up and face down, what you think each one meant in the context of the reading, and what your general impressions were.

Even if a reading makes no sense to you when you do it, its meaning might become clearer later on, and this will encourage you to pay closer attention to your instincts (even if you are sure you're wrong).

Colors of Runes and Their Meaning

In addition to each rune having a meaning, the material in which the runes are carved can color the reading. Most people consistently use runes made of ceramic, stone, or wood

Gold runes - are used for questions about business, career, and property

Jade runes - are used for questions about love, friendship, and relationships.

Ice runes - are used for questions about struggle, conflict, and achievement.

Spirit runes - are used for questions about mysticism, spirituality, and religion.

Stone runes - are used for questions about the natural world and things beyond human control.

Amethyst runes - are used for partnership, protection, love, success and growth.

Using a Casting Cloth or Ground Cloth

This step is as important as the runes themselves.

A ground cloth, or casting cloth will determine how each rune is read.

Beginners and those doing runes and/or a ground for the first time might consider waiting until you are more familiar with both runes and ground.

Others may have a druid ground their runes to a cloth on their behalf. Once the runes are 'grounded' do not use them on any other surface than the ground cloth.

Some ground cloths are very beautiful. Some are quite simple.

The four basic circles and the four elements or directions are present the ground cloth will work.

The more elaborate the drawing on the ground cloth, the more difficult it will be for the reader to determine the true placement of the runes.

Even the most minor miscalculation can greatly impact the final results of a reading.

For this reason, many choose work with a simple ground cloth, so that they may concentrate on the runes.

The basic rune cloth, or ground, consists of material onto which is drawn three circles.

Any material may be used so long as it is durable, soft and of natural material.

Leather works better than cotton because it will last longer and provides better protection for the runes stones when they are thrown on a hard surface.

Cotton backed by quilting or any other insulating material will work just as well.

Do not use glue on any item that will come in contact with the runes.

· Circle 1 - the center circle is where the reading begins. This is referred to as circle 1 - the self. The innermost self, representing what is held secret or sacred.

· Circle 2 - the circle of relationships and life path. These are those people who are in your life and effecting your life on a day-to-day basis.

· Circle 3 - the circle of elemental forces and external influences - spirit guides. The symbols within the third circle represent the four elements and the four directions. Air, earth, water, fire and east, south, west, north. These directions and elements are not fixed. This area represents events that effect more than just you, such as; the weather, politics, taxes, etc. The elements will influence everything in life. When we work with these energies, things are not necessarily easier, but they do move along much more quickly and support is more evident.

· Circle 4 - may or may not be in a circle are four rune symbols. These symbols are not assigned. It is what binds the chosen runes to this particular cloth. Once the runes are bound to the cloth they are considered 'grounded' and therefore the cloth is called the 'ground'. This is the circle of karma. The rune symbols that are placed in the corners of the ground cloth define both the cloth itself and the karma of the reading.

When one or more runes are thrown off the cloth entirely they will be read as representing past lives.

Anything that is not on the cloth indicates either a lesson learned from a past life, or one that is being repeated here.

Which is true depends on the rune and the quadrant of karma.

Methods of Rune Divination

Since there are no reliable historical descriptions of runic divination, virtually any method one chooses can be considered valid.

However, certain characteristics of the runes make them better suited to some methods than others.

For example, most runes are carved onto small bits of wood, clay or stone. These are better designed to be picked up and scattered, rather than being laid out in a specific pattern like the Tarot.

This is verified by descriptions of runic divination in Norse literature, all of which refer to them being 'thrown', 'cast' or 'scattered'.

In the world of divination, we're familiar with things like tarot card readings and sessions with psychic readers, but few people are familiar with rune casting.

Rune casting is different from your standard fortune telling in that it works deeply with your subconscious.

The pouch that holds the rune represents the universe and each symbol etched on each stone represents pieces of that universe.

When you ask a question of your fortune teller your entire mind, both conscious and unconscious, becomes focused on that question.

When performing a runic reading, much like tarot cards the kind of reading performed depends a great deal on the question.

There are different readings for different situations, and the type of rune spread chosen can have a large impact on your question's outcome.

The most important thing, however, is that you feel comfortable with the method you choose.

If you feel the need for a more structured reading than a simple cast provides, devise a pattern for your casting cloth that has some meaning for you to give the reading a more tangible context.

If you find nine or twelve runes to be a bit overwhelming, use three or four.

If you want to just grab a handful and cast them, go right ahead.

The runes themselves should tell you how they want to be read.

You'll find that soon enough you'll lean towards a certain way of casting.

Different sizes, shapes and materials lend themselves to different methods, and through meditation and experimentation you should be able to choose a technique that best suits both the runes personality and your own.

Just make sure your method is consistent. But in the beginning, familiarize yourself with at least a few different options.

Some people end up creating their own unique method of reading the runes.

When you read the example spreads – you will notice there is a wide amount of flexibility given.

The One Rune Method (Odin's Rune)

The runic equivalent of the single card draw in tarot, Odin's rune is the spread to go to if you're looking for a general overview of an entire situation.

The rune chosen will encompass the past, present and future of your issue or question and also cover your potential actions that lead to a potential outcome.

This method is designed to provide a quick, concise answer to a specific question.

It is a great way to begin your day and also build familiarity with your runes.

It can also be used daily as a subject for meditation, or as a general overview of the day before you go to bed.

Think of a specific question.

Then pull a rune from your rune pouch and look at it.

The answer may be an obvious yes or no, or the rune might provide a more conditional response.

If the rune you picked seems to make no sense at all as a response to your question, log it in your journal for review in a few days.

You may then decide to ask another question and in a few days ask the original question again and see if the second reading (which you will also log) sheds more light on the question.

Layout Example One Rune Reading Odin's Rune

One Rune Reading Odin's Rune

The Norns (The Three Rune Method)

The Norn Spread is used to plot the crucial elements of past, present, and future, and to reveal the evolution of the situation through the arc of time.

The left rune represents an important element of the past.

The middle rune represents a deciding element of the present.

The right rune represents the critical element of the future.

This method is helpful in getting an overall read on a given situation and providing some idea about a future outcome.

How much information you get out of it will depend on how much time you spend analyzing the reading and how well you understand the runes.

Pull one rune and lay it down face up.

This rune represents the first Norn - those events in the past which affect the current situation.

Pull another rune and lay it next to the first. This is the second Norn - the present situation, which frequently to a choice that needs to be made.

Pull a third and lay it down. This is the third Norn, and the most difficult rune to interpret.

In some cases, it might represent the person's inevitable fate. In others, it might simply be the end result if the current situation remains unchanged, or even just one of several results.

You will rely on your instincts to decide which is the case.

Remember to log your readings in your journal for future reference.

Layout Example The Norns Three Rune Reading

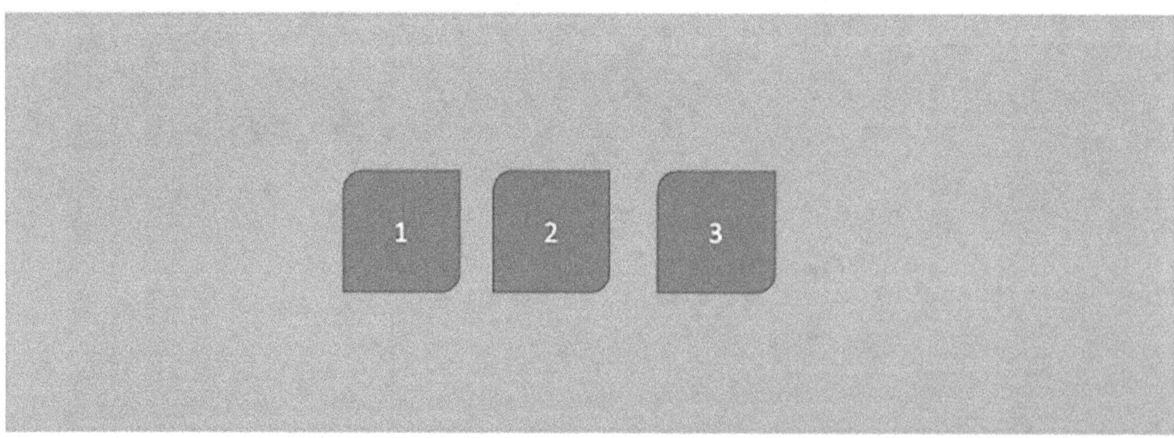

Three Rune Reading   The Three Norns

The Roman Method

This is the method described by Tacitus in Germania.

The method itself is really another variation of the Three-Rune Spread, with a few ritual details to lend it authenticity.

Even if this is not a method that you use, it is good to have a glimpse back in time and imagine those who did these steps 2,000 years ago.

Locate a fruit-bearing tree and use wood from the tree to carve your runes fresh each time.

Lay out a white cloth on the ground.

Take all of the runes in your hands and scatter them.

Invoking the aid of Odin, and without looking at the runes, pick three at random.

You may look at them as a group, without considering them in any particular order, or you can pick them one at a time, using the 'Norns' method described above to interpret them.

(Note – there is not a layout example for this reading as the runes are tossed so each reading will be totally unique in rune placement)

The Nine Rune Cast

This method will give a detailed overview of a person's situation, providing insight into where they are in terms of their spiritual path, clarifying the options and possible outcomes available to them.

Nine is a somewhat arbitrary number - you may use any number that feels comfortable to you.

Nine is commonly used as its multiples were magically significant numbers to the also it is a large enough number to provide a detailed reading, but not so large that it over-complicates things.

It is also easy for most people to hold nine runes in their hands.

Pick nine runes from the pouch.

Hold them between your hands for a moment and focus on your question (if you have one).

Then scatter the runes on the table, floor, or cloth if you have one.

Read the runes which land face up first.

These will relate to the current situation and the circumstances, which led to it.

How the runes are read is largely subjective, but in general, runes lying in the center are the most immediately relevant, while those lying around the edges are less important, or represent more general influences.

Runes that are close together or even touching often complement each other, or may even represent a single thing, while runes which fall on opposite sides of the pattern frequently represent opposing influences.

Occasionally, a rune will land completely off the cloth or fall off the table.

Some people consider such runes to be particularly significant, while others ignore them completely.

Once you have looked at the runes which landed face up, turn over the rest without moving them from their positions.

These represent outside or future influences and will point to possible outcomes.

It is up to you to decide what the various positions and patterns in a reading mean, but once you have come up with a few general rules, try to stick with them.

However, rune readings by their nature are fluid, subjective things so try not to impose too much order on your readings.

Your runes are unique, like snowflakes and like people.

Just look at the patterns and relationships that appear in each reading and see what interpretations make sense to you.

Later when you look back upon past readings that you logged in your journal, you may see a pattern.

Once you have completed the reading, you can then pull one more rune from your pouch.

This single rune may help confirm (or dispute) your conclusions drawn from the reading.

It also helps you to focus and drill down on a reading that was complicated.

(Note – there is not a layout diagram for this reading as the runes are tossed. Each reading layout will be uniquely different)

The Runic Cross

The Runic Cross gives you an in-depth analysis of any problem.

The Runic Cross is the most complex of the traditional spreads.

This is your go-to if you want an in-depth analysis of the situation that you've found yourself in.

Ask your question out loud and six runes will be drawn and placed down in the shape of a cross, with four runes going up and down and then one rune placed on either side of the second rune from the top.

The rune on the right represents the past, the second rune from the bottom is you now and the rune on the far left is what's in store for you in the future.

The rune at the very bottom will tell you the basis, or foundation, of the issue and the second rune from the top tells you what obstacles are in store for you.

Finally, the top rune will reveal the best outcome in store for you after overcoming those obstacles.

Layout Example The Runic Cross

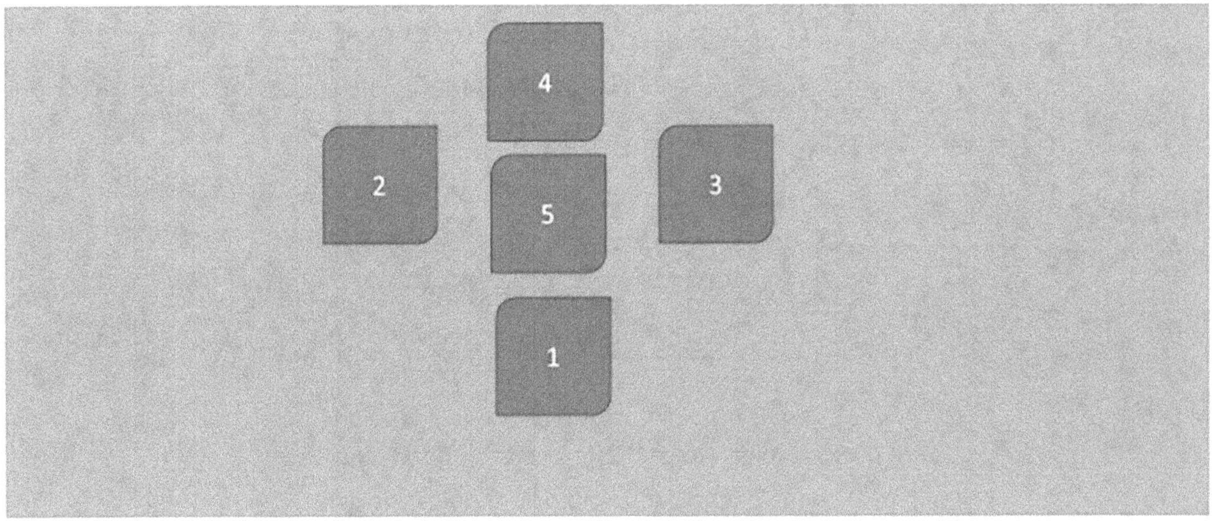

Five Rune Reading   The Runic Cross

The Three Rune Cast

With the three rune cast you may be thinking that it's comparable to the three card tarot draw.

Visually it is; you ask a question and pull out three runes, placing them down in a line.

But that's where the similarity ends.

The first rune to the right describes the situation for you, or more specifically the issues that need addressing within the situation.

The middle rune will suggest a course of action that may assist in resolving it.

The final rune on the left tells you what outcome will be the result of the action chosen on the middle rune.

Layout Example Three Rune Cast

Three Rune Reading   The Three Norns

Celestial Spread

The celestial spread is a yearly (13 runes needed) spread - starting with the month you are in now.

Runes chosen 1 -12 are set up in a diamond shape starting with the right and ending up with rune 12 at the top of the diamond.

The last or 13th rune should be placed in the middle.

Rune 1 should be month 1 and so on.

The 13th rune should be the final and should represent the influence for the year.

Layout Example Celestial Spread

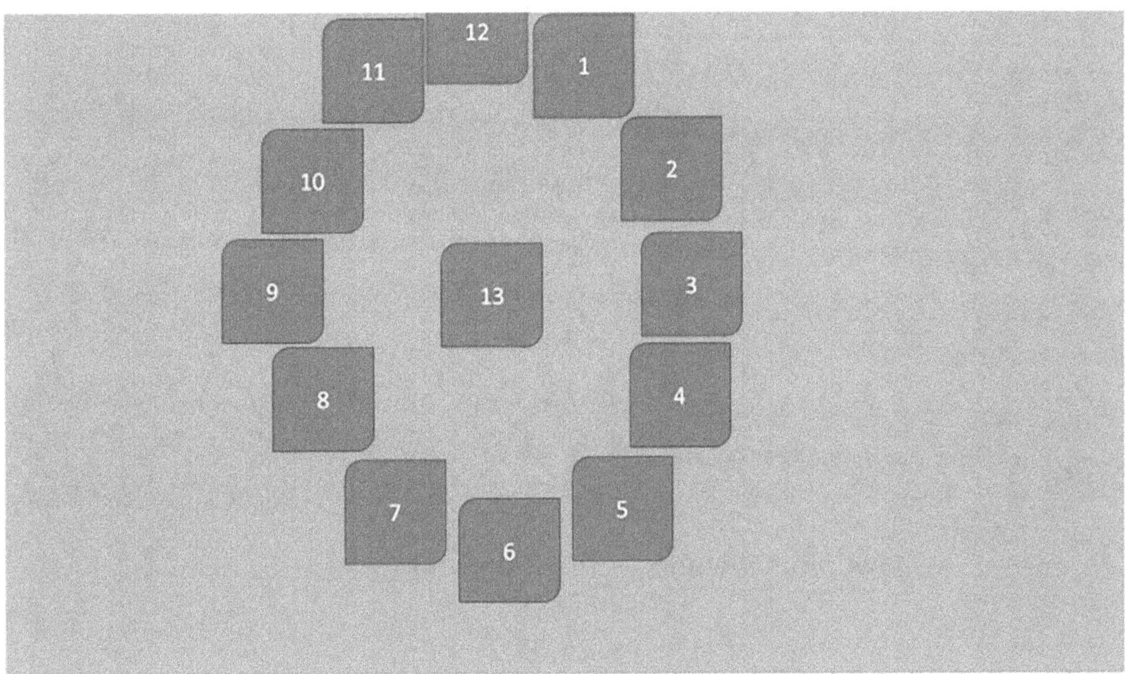

Thirteen Rune Reading   The Celestial Spread

Diamond Spread

The diamond spread reveals the dynamic forces at work in a situation.

It is the spread of choice for understanding a hidden conflict.

The bottom rune represents the foundation that forms the basis of the issue.

The left rune represents one of the forces acting on the issue at hand.

The right rune represents another of the forces acting on the issue at hand.

The top rune represents the conclusion to which your strivings can carry you.

Layout Example Diamond Spread

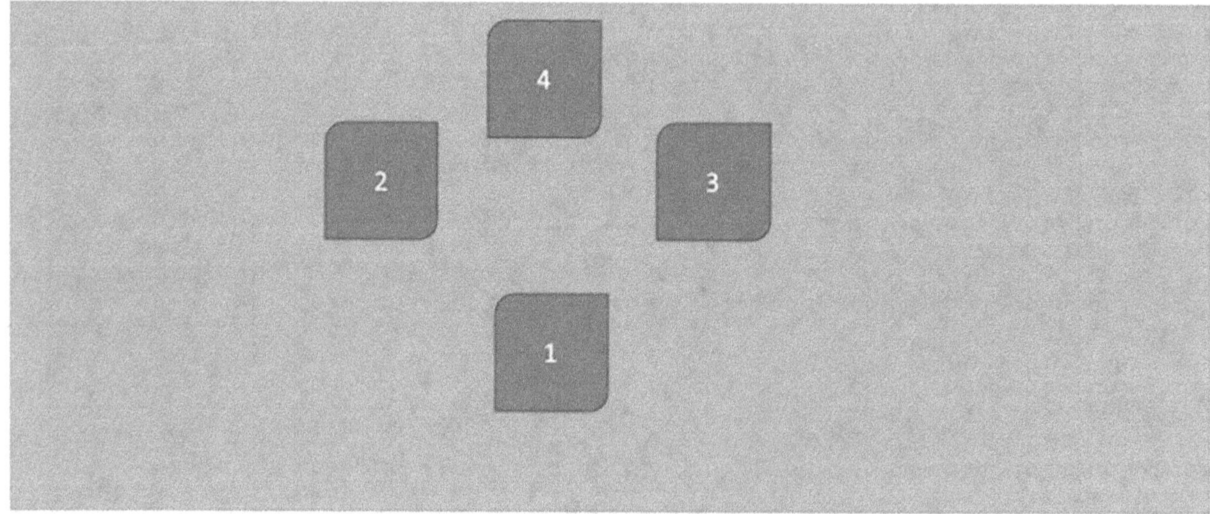

Four Rune Reading   The Diamond Spread

Elemental Spread

The elements spread shows the four elements and their corresponding qualities.

The top rune, earth is lessons to be learned on the physical plane.

The right rune; air, lessons to be learned on the mental plane.

The bottom rune; fire, lessons to be learned on the spiritual plane.

The left rune; water, lessons to be learned on the emotional plane.

Layout Example The Elemental Spread

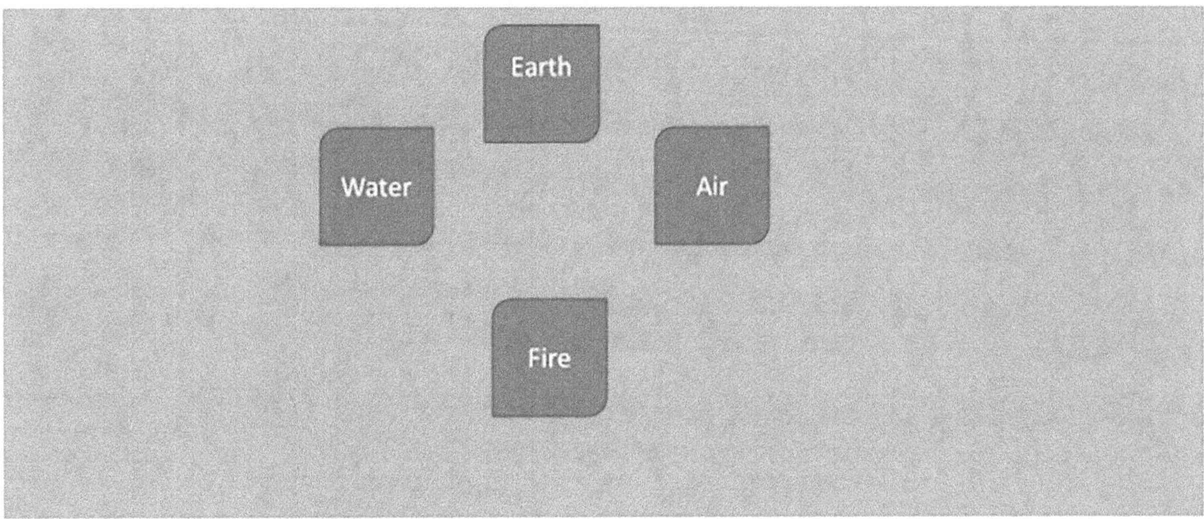

Four Rune Reading   The Elemental Spread

Fork Spread

The fork spread is used at critical turning points, to understand the dynamics of an important decision.
    The left rune represents the first possible outcome.
    The right rune represents the second possible outcome.
    The bottom rune represents the critical factor that determines what will come to pass.

Layout Example The Fork Spread

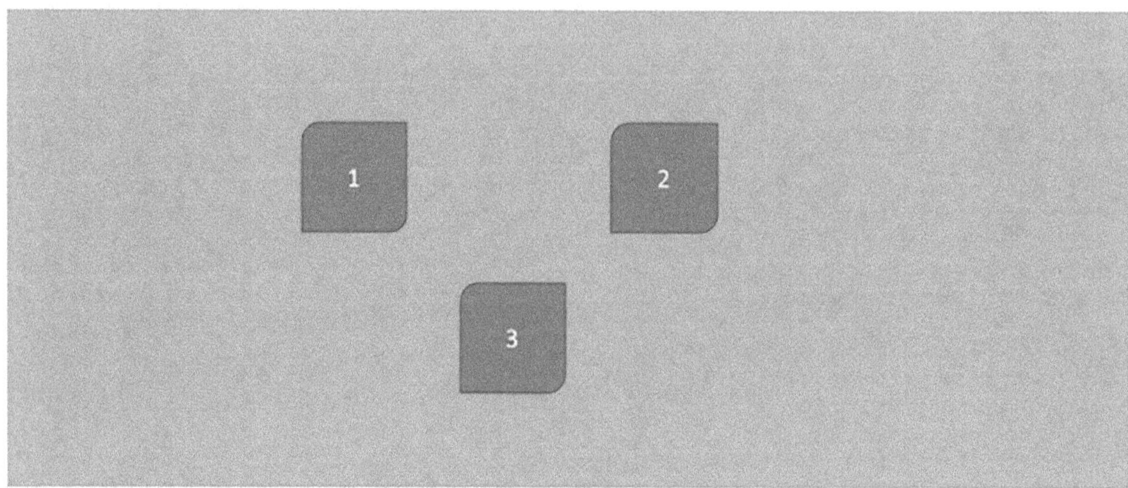

Three Reading   The Fork Spread

Medicine Wheel Spread

Medicine wheel spread is a five-rune cast to give guidance to a specific problem when the questioner does not know which path to follow.

The left sided rune deals with the past or source of the problem.

The right rune represents the present or current influences.

The bottom rune deals with the future or the way energies are flowing.

The top rune shows the challenge.

The center rune represents the power to call upon.

Layout Example Medicine Wheel Spread

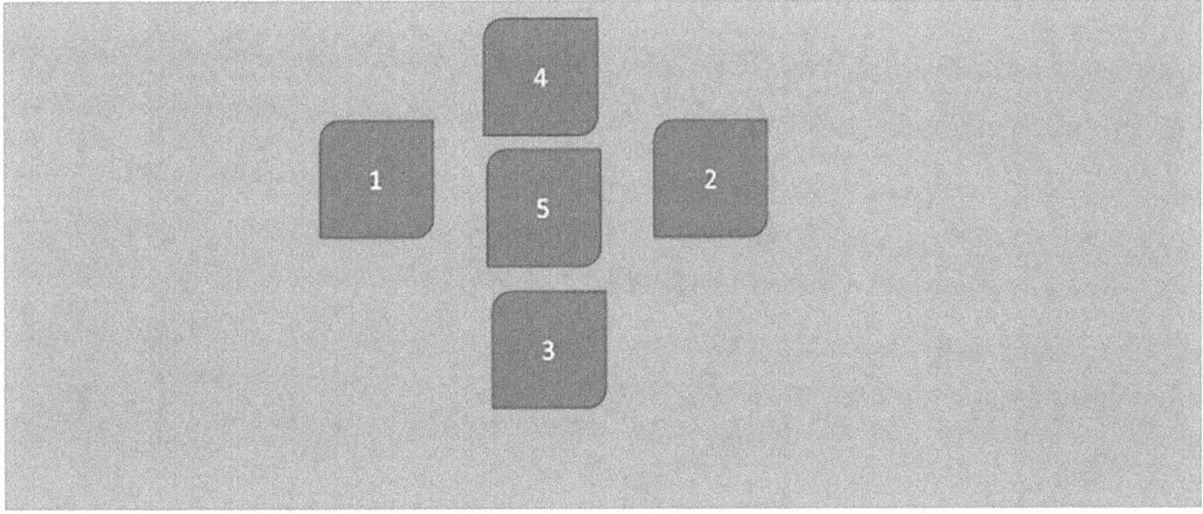

Five Rune Reading   The Medicine Wheel Spread

Relationship Spread

The Relationship spread is very useful to get an understanding of the purpose of people who are partners.

It shows the role of each person in the other person's life and the potential direction of the relationship.

Rune #1: this rune represents the energy or attitude towards the relationship of the person asking the question.

Rune #2: this one represents the partner's energy or attitude about the relationship.

Rune #3: the third rune shows how the partnership is doing or what the purpose of the people being together is.

Layout Example Relationship Spread

Relationship Spread Three Rune Reading

Closing

Thank you for taking the time to purchase and read through this book. I hope you have found your beginning rune journey to be interesting and enjoyable.

You may have noticed some of the rune spreads did not have a diagram for an example. If the runes are cast (tossed) – we have no way of knowing what we will see each reading. With that being said, I left out examples on a couple spreads as each time you do that spread it will be unique. I hope this makes sense as I explained.

I've added a couple pages following this page in case you wanted to jot down notes for later reference.

Notes

Notes

Notes

Notes

Notes

Notes

Notes

Notes

Notes

Notes

www.ingramcontent.com/pod-product-compliance
Lightning Source LLC
Chambersburg PA
CBHW060202120726
48004CB00007B/1660